Understanding Plagiarism

A Student Guide to Writing Your Own Work

Rosemarie Menager-Beeley, Ed.D.

Foothill College

Lyn Paulos

Santa Barbara City College

HOUGHTON MIFFLIN COMPANY
Boston New York

Vice President and Publisher: Patricia A. Coryell
Editor-in-Chief: Suzanne Phelps Weir
Senior Sponsoring Editor: Lisa Kimball
Development Manager: Sarah Helyar Chester
Editorial Associate: Peter Mooney
Editorial Assistant: Brett Pasinella
Manufacturing Coordinator: Priscilla Manchester
Senior Marketing Manager: Cindy Graff Cohen

Printed in the U.S.A.

ISBN: 0-618-66297-9

56789-EB-09 08 07 06

Contents

1
Introduction

What is in this guide?

This booklet is designed to help students avoid the pitfalls of plagiarism. Chapters cover the correct way to credit sources, quote, cite, paraphrase, summarize, create a list of references, and more. Knowledge checks are provided at the end of each chapter to give you an opportunity to practice the skills presented in this booklet.

Why is this guide important to you as a student?

What do you want from college? You probably want to succeed in your classes. The last thing you want is to fail a class for cheating or plagiarizing by mistake. If you are unfamiliar with the practices and rules of incorporating work from other sources, then you will find this guide a useful resource.

Citing correctly can be confusing, but we've tried to make it as clear and simple as possible. Most colleges have very specific requirements about giving references, depending on the subject or instructor. Citing correctly is more involved than inserting footnotes or listing references at the end of a paper. This guide provides information and samples of the kinds of citations that are necessary to correctly reference different types of academic work.

What is plagiarism?

Plagiarism is using someone else's work and passing it off as one's own. The term comes from the Latin word *plagiarius*, which means *kidnapper*.

This means that if a student uses another writer's work without giving credit, it may be considered deceptive even if it is an honest mistake. Knowing the definition of plagiarism and when to cite sources is the best way to avoid problems.

Why should you credit another author's work?

When you enter an institution of higher learning, you become part of a community of writers, researchers, and thinkers who value scholarship and academic integrity. If you claim another author's writing as your own, you are essential stealing his or her intellectual property. As John Van Rys, one of the author's of *The College Writer's Handbook*, notes, this hurts your standing in the academic community. You are being disrespectful of other writers and researchers. You are also disrespecting your readers when you pass others' ideas off as your own. As well, when you plagiarize, you harm the reputation and integrity of your college (486).

When should you credit another author's work?

Because many things such as information, pictures, and music are now so easy to copy from the Internet, it's more tempting than ever to find and use those materials for free. How can you tell when it is appropriate to use something without a citation and when it isn't?

Generally any time you use someone else's work as a source of ideas or inspiration, credit is required. There are a few exceptions, such as when the information is common knowledge. An example of common knowledge is the fact that Christopher Columbus crossed the Atlantic Ocean in 1492. To be safe, if you consult a source and that source's ideas become part of your work, then you need to cite that source. If you use a direct quotation, then you need to reproduce it accurately and to cite it correctly. These practices will prevent inadvertent plagiarizing, and this guide will provide the basics to get you started.

Tip

When you consult a source, cite it correctly!

There are also limitations to how much of someone else's work can be used as part of an assignment. Exclusively, excessively, or inappropriately using another author's work by copying, paraphrasing, summarizing, or directly quoting is plagiarizing. It is important to use your own words and ideas in a paper. One suggested rule of thumb for acceptable use of content in a submitted assignment is up to 10 percent, provided it is properly cited (Zaharoff). Make sure to check your instructor's preferences.

Many students worry that their writing does not sound as professional as that of the original author. But that fear ignores the point of using a source in the first place. Instructors do not give assignments so students can give them back another author's work. Instructors do not expect the same quality of work from a novice as from an expert. College is a place of learning. If instructors wanted to read only the professional author's words and ideas, they could go directly to the original source and skip the student's work.

The whole point of having you use sources is to enable you to learn from those sources and to develop your own writing and analytical skills. It's important for you to work with ideas and to express them in writing so you can develop your own writing style, perspective, and voice. This is a big investment of time and effort. Often when students risk plagiarizing, they haven't allowed themselves sufficient time to complete an assignment. These types of miscalculations can lead to trouble.

Know the rules.

Because academic honesty and the validity of a college degree are vitally important to institutions of higher learning, schools create codes or policies governing instances of dishonesty. Many of these policies are listed as Academic Integrity, Academic Honesty, Honor Code, Cheating, Student Conduct Code, or Plagiarism. The codes may consist of a list of rules, definitions, specific behaviors, procedures, and consequences of academic dishonesty. **It is your responsibility to know the rules of your institution and to follow them.** Rules are usually published in school catalogs and considered a part of the enrollment

---

Tip

Know the rules about plagiarism; ignorance is no excuse.

---

agreement for the college. If you have any questions about academic policies, then check with your instructor or the dean's office to get the facts.

When instructors suspect plagiarism, they will follow steps prescribed by the institution to address the problem. These steps include contacting the student and forwarding a report to the dean or a disciplinary committee, which will probably conduct a hearing.

Consequences to the student can include failing the assignment or the course, as well as being given community service or some other restitution to the campus community. Some students have been unhappily surprised to learn that the consequences for a first-time offense of plagiarism can be as severe as expulsion from the institution. Being caught as a plagiarizer is humiliating, can directly affect your progress toward a degree, is costly, and is entirely avoidable.

Knowledge Check: True or False?

1. Most students who plagiarize do so inadvertently.
2. Students cannot be accused of plagiarizing if they don't know the citation style expected by the instructor.
3. Using sources for educational purposes means that those sources are exempt from citation rules.

Answers

1. (True) Don't be one of them. This can be a costly mistake!
2. (False) It is your job to find out.
3. (False) All sources should be cited.

2
How to Avoid Plagiarism

12 Tips to Avoid Plagiarizing

1. Do your own work, and use your own words.
2. Allow yourself enough time to research the assignment.
3. Keep careful track of your sources
4. Take careful notes.
5. Assemble your thoughts, and make clear who is speaking.
6. If you use an idea, a quotation, paraphrase, or summary, then credit the source.
7. Learn how to cite sources correctly both in the body of your paper and in your List of Works Cited.
8. Quote accurately and sparingly.
9. Paraphrase carefully.
10. Do not patchwrite.
11. Summarize, don't auto-summarize.
12. Do not rework another student's paper or buy a paper from a paper-mill.

Do your own work, and use your own words.

College gives you the opportunity to be exposed to new ideas, to formulate ideas of your own, and to develop skills to communicate your ideas. Strengthening your writing skills requires hard work and practice, but you will learn thinking and communicating skills that will benefit both your studies in college and your career.

Expressing a thought in your own words may seem overwhelming. The difficulty may stem from not understanding the language, not understanding the research material, or a lack of confidence in expressing ideas and concepts. Don't be discouraged that your paper may not sound as professional as you would like. By creating and practicing your own personal style, you will improve your ability to state ideas clearly and support arguments, and your vocabulary will increase.

These skills are not built by using another researcher's or student's words or by paying a service to write a paper for your class. Attempting to cheat on your paper cheats you the most because you are depriving yourself of the thinking, learning, and writing practice that would have benefited all of your classwork and beyond. But cheating also creates the risk of humiliation and punishment. Most professors are so familiar with the work in their field that they can spot a fake quickly. New plagiarism detection methods are also making it easier for professors to catch cheaters electronically. And as discussed in Chapter 1, all institutions will punish students who plagiarize. Doing honest work is the way to avoid the humiliation of being accused of cheating.

Allow yourself enough time to research the assignment.

Plagiarism is most tempting when you haven't allowed yourself enough time to complete the assignment. You can avoid such temptation by giving yourself plenty of time to complete all the steps necessary for the assignment: selecting the topic, doing the research, then writing and refining your ideas. Minimizing the time it will take to do the work, or procrastinating because you feel that you do better work when you are anxious, will easily create trouble.

The most productive strategy is to begin the assignment as soon as it is given and try to complete it early. This allows you to adjust the schedule if you encounter any research difficulties, provides time for questions or clarification, and offsets other events that can interfere or cut into study time. If you are unsure about how to plot out your time for each step, then ask your instructor to help you plan your schedule.

Keep careful track of your sources.

As you look through books, articles, and electronic materials, you will be able to identify which content is relevant to your paper. The sources that you decide to take notes from are the ones you will need to keep careful records of.

Create a master list of all your sources that contains detailed bibliographic information for each item. (You will need to record the author; title of article or book; publisher, periodical title, electronic medium, or URL; date, and page number. See Chapters 6 or 7 for a detailed list of the information you will need and the format you will need to provide it in.) As you conduct your research, you will likely add or delete sources from this list, but keeping it current and complete will make your work much easier when it comes time to format the list into your formal list of Works Cited (for MLA papers) or References list (for

APA papers). This list of sources will enable the readers of your paper to locate the exact content you discuss in your paper, as well as to assist you to find it again, should you need to.

Take careful notes.

Some students find they take more complete notes (and can easily refer back to their sources) if they make photocopies of the relevant pages from their sources. If you decide to use this method, for print sources, such as articles and books, copy the copyright page and relevant content pages of each source. Make sure the page numbers or other identifiers are visible on each page. For electronic sources, such as the Web sites, databases, CDs, or even blogs, print out both the home or copyright page and the relevant content pages, making sure that identifiers such as the URL and the date, or page numbers, are visible.

If you take notes on note cards or in computer files, then make sure to keep a detailed record of where each note came from and take down the information carefully and accurately.

Next scrutinize your resources, thinking about the ideas expressed, noting and recording the relevant points, and adding to the notes your reactions, questions, and thoughts. If you find a particular phrasing that you want to quote, then highlight it to separate it from the regular notes.

Assemble your thoughts, and make clear who is speaking.

As you write the first draft of your paper, make sure you are expressing your thoughts and ideas in your own voice. Use the thoughts or words of others *only to support* your own thoughts, *not to make your point for you.* Your writing should make clear at all times who is speaking.

If you are using material from one of your researched sources, you can present it in one of three ways: quoting, summarizing, or paraphrasing. These methods are discussed in Chapters 3, 4, and 5.

If you use an idea, a quotation, paraphrase, or summary, then credit the source.

When you draft your paper, if you are stating another person's thought, make clear where that thought came from. Identify the source of all borrowed content in your paper, even if it's from a blog on the Internet. Your readers need to know where to find the original source if they want to explore the idea further.

Identify your source by inserting a brief parenthetical citation in the paper where the source's content appears, and then list the complete source information at the end of the paper. Follow the documentation style directed by your instructor (usually MLA or APA; see Chapters 6 or 7 for examples.)

Cite sources correctly, both in the body of your paper and in your list of Works Cited or References.

A citation—that is, stating the source of an idea, a conclusion, or a specific collection of information—of another person's work is the highest form of respect that a serious writer can make. It is also the single best way to avoid accusations of plagiarism and cheating. Properly citing sources involves acknowledging them both in the body of your work (when and where your writing borrows from a given source) and in a list of all the sources at the end of your paper.

Citation styles differ by subject or discipline. There are styles for English, the Social Sciences, the Humanities, and the Sciences. Check with your instructor or writing center for the proper format style of your writing project.

See Chapters 6 and 7 for basic models of citations in both MLA and APA documentation styles. Style guides such as the *MLA Handbook for Writers of Research Papers* (sixth edition) and the *Publication Manual of the American Psychological Association* (fifth edition), which are available in most bookstores, provide models for all common types of sources. Online citation generators (see Chapter 9) can also help you with listing references in the correct format.

Quote accurately and sparingly.

Quotations should be used *only to emphasize your own point*, which you have already stated in your own words. A good quotation from an original source can underscore a theme and introduce thoughts or direction, but quotations should be relevant, necessary, accurate, and limited.

Using too many direct quotations (more than 10 percent) is a sign that you have not developed your own ideas enough and that you are relying on others to make your point for you. Over-quoting is also an opportunity for plagiarism to creep in. If you are using several sources, then limit how much those sources contribute, and give correct citations and credit every time you use them.

Paraphrase carefully.

Sometimes paraphrasing inadvertently becomes plagiarism. You might think you are paraphrasing when you take another writer's sentence and then look up words and replace them with synonyms (see Chapter 4), however merely changing some of another writer's words, or reversing the order of the clauses in the sentences, is still plagiarism. When you paraphrase, you must state in your own words what another writer believes or argues.

Do not patchwrite.

Patchwriting consists of mixing several references together and arranging paraphrases and quotations to constitute much of a paper. In essence, the student has assembled others' works with a bit of embroidery here and there but with very little original thinking or expression. Turning in work that has been woven into a quilt with patches arranged together constitutes plagiarism. Instead, work on developing a position and bringing in sources to support the viewpoint or argument that you are presenting.

A way to avoid patchwriting is good preparation. Read the material several times to make sure you understand what the source is saying; then put it aside and think about it. Reread the material and annotate it—noting important points in the margins or highlighting parts of the material that support your own ideas. You might even organize the main points of the reading into an outline to help you better understand the ideas presented.

Summarize, don't auto-summarize.

Most word processors have an automatic summarize function that can take fifty pages and turn them into ten. The problem with this feature is that it condenses material by selecting key sentences. Therefore a summarized version is still in the exact words of the original source, only shorter and not necessarily making the same point as the original. The auto-summary feature is intended for writers to summarize their *own* work, *not* the work of others. If a student uses any portion of the auto-summary from another writer's work, then it is plagiarism.

If you wish to summarize another writer's work, then describe briefly in your own words the writer's idea (identifying who that writer is and providing a citation to the work) and state how it relates to your own ideas. (See Chapter 5.)

Do not rework another student's paper or buy a paper from a paper mill.

Don't cross the line from looking at someone else's paper as an example of how to do the assignment, to the action of using it as original work. Reworking someone else's paper is plagiarism. It also shows that a student is unwilling to think for him- or herself.

Similarly, buying papers from paper mills, or paying for someone else to write a paper, is obviously dishonest and is a clear example of plagiarizing and cheating. Databases of written papers are often kept by colleges and by plagiarism detection services such as www.turnitin.com, so instructors who have a question about the authenticity of a student's paper can easily verify its source.

Knowledge Check: True or False?

1. One way to avoid plagiarizing is to give yourself enough time to do a good job on the assignment.
2. As long as you put everything in quotation marks, you are not plagiarizing.
3. Getting a paper from a friend or the Internet is a good way to get a head start on your assignment.

Answers

1. (True) Most people who plagiarize use poor time management and even worse judgment.
2. (False) If you quote more than 10 percent of your paper, you may be graded down for over-quoting.
3. (False) Using a friend's paper or an Internet paper is plagiarizing and considered to be academic cheating.

3
Using Quotations

A **direct quotation** is a word-for-word repetition from another source. Using quotations is an effective way to support your arguments and add credibility to your research paper. Quotations are most useful when they highlight or help to refine a point you are making. Inserting too many quotations in your paper distracts your readers from the argument you are trying to construct, and makes your paper sound as if you are letting others speak for you, so use quotations selectively and sparingly.

Each time you insert a direct or indirect quotation into your paper, you must add a citation to the source at the quotation. This in-text citation follows an abbreviated, parenthetical format that points your reader to the full citation in a Works Cited or References list at the end of your paper (see Chapter 6 or 7).

Quotations can be used in various ways within a research paper. This chapter will cover some of those uses and the proper citation styles needed for each. Follow these basic rules for using quotations:

- Use quotations sparingly.
- Make sure the quotation exactly fits the idea of your paragraph.
- Make sure direct quotations stay identical to the original passage. Do not change the wording, the spelling, or the punctuation of the original passage.

- Cite the source! Include a parenthetical citation for all quotations.
- If a direct quotation is longer than four lines, use a block quotation.

How do you use direct quotations?

A direct quotation is an exact copy of the original author's work. Make your point first, and then enclose the quote in quotation marks (or if it is long set it apart as a block quotation) and provide a parenthetical citation directly after.

Example: parenthetical citation, MLA

The MLA style of citing a quotation includes the author's last name followed by the page number directly after the quotation. Note that no comma separates the name from the page number.

Personal growth is a painful process, and part of that process is taking personal responsibility for your actions. This includes remembering that "you can't talk your way out of problems you behaved yourself into" (Covey 186).

Example: parenthetical citation, APA

The APA style of citing the same quotation includes the publication year as well as the author's last name and page number. Note that no comma separates the name from the date, but that a comma does follow the date and that the abbreviation p. precedes the page number.

Personal growth is a painful process, and part of that process is taking personal responsibility for your actions. This includes remembering that "you can't talk your way out of problems you behaved yourself into" (Covey, 1989, p. 186).

Notice that in both cases the citation is included in the sentence, with the period after the citation.

Example: author's name in text, MLA

You can introduce the name of the author in the text and then cite the page number for reference.

Noted author Stephen Covey suggests that to be effective, one must "begin with the end in mind" (97).

Example: author's name in text, APA

Note that the APA style includes the year of publication directly after the author's name and the page number at the end for easy reference.

Weeks (1994) believes that "we need to celebrate diversity, not fear it or perceive it as a threat" (p. 33).

How do you quote a secondary source?

When using research sources it is common to find that
the original author has quoted a **secondary source**,
another author, in his or her work. The following
example shows such a quotation and the proper citation
for it.

Example: secondary source, MLA

The addition of qtd. in (for "quoted in") shows that this
quote by Jung was found in a secondary resource,
written by Byrne.

Psychology has had its masters of theory and quite a
bit of humor as well. C. G. Jung, a noted psychologist,
once claimed, "Show me a sane man and I will cure
him for you." (qtd. in Byrne 453).

Use ellipses to show omissions and brackets to show insertions.

An **ellipsis** (shown by three evenly spaced periods: ...)
is a break or omission of words within a direct quote.
Using only part of a quotation is common practice,
especially if the entire quotation is too long or
cumbersome. But make sure to use ellipses cautiously
so you don't present the author's words out of intended
context.

Example: ellipses to show omitted words from the middle of a quote

We can now plainly and painfully see that "components of human interaction ... often lead to conflict" (Weeks 33).

Example: bracketed insertion to make a sentence correct

Sometimes a quote will be worded in a way that could read awkwardly or make an incomplete sentence when inserted in a paper. If you need to add a word or phrase within a quotation to make your sentence grammatically correct or clearer, then put brackets around your insertion.

There are many examples of how "components of human interaction... [can] often lead to conflict" (Weeks 33).

In this instance the word can was added to clarify the thought for the reader.

Use block quotations for longer quotes.

A quotation from poetry, plays, or any text longer than four lines should be set apart in a block quotation format. A block quotation is indented about one inch (ten spaces) from the left margin and double-spaced. A block quotation needs no quotation marks and is introduced by a complete sentence. Often a colon, rather than a period, follows the introductory words.

> ***Tip***
>
> **Block quotations do not require quotation marks**

Example: block quotation, MLA

The block quotation is introduced by a sentence that contains the author's name, ends with a colon, and uses ellipsis to show that it is not complete. Note that the page number is in parentheses after the period.

As Jess Tavares explains, older students face different challenges when returning to school:

> As an older student, returning to the academic world was quite a shock. I hadn't seen a classroom in twenty-five years. But with a new backpack, pens, and a bill from the bookstore that equaled my rent, I sat in my very first college class, ... scared to death I could not pass the tests I had just set for myself (2).

Example: block quotation, APA

Treat a block quotation for an APA paper the same as you would a block quotation for an MLA paper, except for the citation at the end of the quote. The parenthetical citation should include "p." before the page number.

As Jess Tavares explains, older students face different challenges when returning to school:

> As an older student, returning to the academic world was quite a shock. I hadn't seen a classroom in twenty-five years. But with a new backpack, pens, and a bill from the bookstore that equaled my rent, I sat in my very first college class, ... scared to death I could not pass the tests I had just set for myself (p. 2).

Knowledge Check: True or False?

1. Quotations must be used in original form.
2. Quotation marks are required for all direct quotations.
3. Brackets indicate that a word has been added that is not in the original text.

Answers

1. (True) Quotations should be identical to the original passage.
2. (False) Block quotations do not require quotation marks.
3. (True) Brackets show that text was added to the original passage.

4
Paraphrasing

What is a paraphrase?

A **paraphrase** is a restatement of an author's writing by using your own words to accurately convey the original information. Paraphrase an author's work when you want to explain the content of his or her passage while maintaining your own voice and rhythm. You might also paraphrase after you have introduced a source earlier in your paper and wish to continue to discuss that source's ideas without needing to quote the source verbatim.

The length of a paraphrase should be about equal to the length of the original work.

It is vital that the paraphrase not alter the original meaning of the source. Adding words that distort the intention of the author or leaving out significant parts of what the author was intending misstates that author.

A paraphrase, because it is an indirect quotation, always requires a parenthetical citation. (See the MLA and APA examples below.)

To restate an author's ideas accurately but in your own words and writing style can be difficult. You might be tempted to shift some words around from the original, but doing so would be plagiarizing because those words and the idea still belong to the author. Remember that improving your writing skills is part of the goal of using others' works. Instructors want you to learn to write and think, not just to hand back what someone else has created.

Tips
DO
1. Use your own words.
2. Present the author's ideas without changing, adding to, or deleting from the original meaning.
3. Make the paraphrase about equal in length to the original.
4. Give credit to the source.
DON'T
1. Keep the author's sentences and just replace the words with synonyms.
2. Flip-flop clauses and leave the words the same.
3. Lose track of original sources.

Accuracy is vital.

One way to develop paraphrasing skills is to read the material several times to make sure that you understand completely what the writer is saying. Next, put aside the author's work and try to explain the passage in your own words. This will help you to develop a personal voice and style. Compare the explanation with the original and decide whether it is accurate and conveys the original ideas. Consider whether something is missing that a person who didn't read the first passage would need to know in order to understand it. Make sure to explain for your reader how the paraphrased content relates to your idea. Once

you have worked the paraphrase into your draft, be
sure to cite the original.

Sample paraphrases

Example 1: paraphrase with citation, MLA

Original work

> Poll after poll indicates that one of the primary
> concerns of contemporary U.S. citizens is
> violence. Terrorism is obviously one part of
> this concern, but there is also considerable
> concern about nonterrorist forms of violence.
> Violence among the nation's youth is
> especially troubling and difficult to explain.
> This difficulty is frequently the reason that
> social psychologists are often asked to make
> sense of seemingly senseless acts of violence.
> Why are there so many shootings in the U.S.
> high schools? Why are there so many gangs,
> and why are they growing at such alarming
> rates? (Potter 306)

Incorrect paraphrase

> Survey after survey show that one of the big
> things that people in the U.S. worry about
> today is violence. Terrorism is clearly a
> reason but there is also a lot of worry about
> other forms of violence. Violence from the
> young people in this country is very confusing

> **and** <u>hard</u> **to** <u>understand</u>. **This** <u>problem</u> **is** <u>often</u> **the** <u>issue</u> **that researchers** are <u>frequently required</u> to <u>explain incomprehensible violent crimes. What is the reason for the number of gun related crimes in schools in America? Is it because the number of</u> **gangs** <u>are going up</u>?

In the above example the writing style of the original piece was copied. It was plagiarized, not paraphrased. Sentence by sentence, the information is exactly restated using different words. The substituted words in exact sequence are underlined. The sequence of each idea and structure of each sentence is the same, and words have been replaced with synonyms. In some cases original phrases have been kept in order (shown in bold). This patchwork paraphrasing is the result of using a thesaurus to find synonyms for words in the original text, but everything is essentially identical. Finally, there was no indication of the source of this paraphrase.

Correct paraphrase

According to James Potter, many recent **polls** have suggested that people in the United States are very concerned about **terrorism** and other acts of **violence**. Increasing violence, including **shootings**, among **high-school-**aged children is one of these concerns. People in the community want to understand why this is happening. **Social psychologists** have been asked to explain this troubling trend. It is difficult to understand why young people may be joining **gangs** and committing acts of violence in greater numbers (Potter 306).

This example maintains the ideas of the original piece, but the style of writing is different. Instead of following an identical sequence to the original work, the correctly paraphrased paragraph conveys the information but does not pull out words and substitute them with synonyms. It uses some of the words from the original to accurately present the author's ideas and is complete in presenting the original author's ideas, but it uses the student's own original sentences. It also cites the author of the original work.

Example 2: paraphrase with citation, APA

Original work

> At first glance, there appears to be little justification for telling the story of California's early Indian wars. Aside from the brief Modoc conflict of 1873, and possibly the Mariposa war of 1851, few people are aware that California had any Indian troubles during the Gold Rush days of the 1850's. Certainly the Far West never had a Custer's Last Stand or a grand retreat such as that made by Chief Joseph of the Nez Perce. Here were no Sitting

Bull or Geronimo, no spectacular uprisings, like Adobe Walls or Beecher's Islands. On the contrary, many California tribes were generally peaceful by nature, few having even a war club or a tomahawk as part of their culture. Yet in California, the bloodiest drama in the settlement of the West took place, a brutal disruption and destruction so devastating that by the 1870's many native groups were extinct. (Secrest, 2003)

Incorrect paraphrase

Unless you know about the events, you would think there isn't much reason to write about what happened in the **Indian wars** in **early California**. There were two conflicts, one in **1873** with the **Modoc** and another in **Mariposa in 1851**. But most people don't know anything about California having trouble with Indians during the 1850's Gold Rush. The **Far West** didn't have any famous Indian conflicts like **Custer's Last Stand** or any other Indians that were well known like **Chief Joseph of the Nez Perce, Sitting Bull, or Geronimo**. It didn't have Indian revolts like **Adobe Walls or Beecher's Islands**. In California the Indians were peaceful and didn't carry weapons. But

<u>California had the</u> **bloodiest** <u>wars in the</u> **West**.
<u>It was harsh and destructive and annihilated
the Indians to the point where by the 1870's
many of the groups were dead and gone.</u>

This paragraph is plagiarized. Notice that the writing
style of the original piece was copied. Sentence by
sentence the information is restated using different
words, and the sequence of each idea and sentence is
the same. In most cases, words have been substituted
for synonyms (see underlined). In some cases words
have been kept (see bold). This is another example of
patchwork paraphrasing. In addition, no indication of
the source of this paraphrase is provided in the text.

Correct paraphrase

As historian William Secrest (2003) notes, if history
books are to be believed, there is little to say about the
California Indian conflicts. Indeed it would seem that all
of the great battles such as Custer's Last Stand and
the great chiefs took place far away. While history
shows us the Gold Rush and its effect on California, it
also leaves us with the false impression that California
Indians were peaceful, with no weapons or conflicts
with the intruding whites. This type of historical
omission negates the devastation and annihilation that
the California Indians suffered, Secrest explains;

annihilation so complete "that by the 1870's many native groups were extinct" (pg. xi).

In this example the ideas of the original piece are maintained, but the style of writing is different and belongs to the writer of the paper. Instead of following an identical sequence to the original work, the correctly paraphrased paragraph conveys the information but does not pull out words and substitute them with synonyms. It still uses some of the phrasing from the original, but this instance is identified by quotation marks and is used to accurately convey and emphasize the ideas of the original author. It also cites the author of the original work.

To avoid the errors of adding information that wasn't in the original work or omitting something important to the original meaning, carefully track your sources and acknowledge them in your writing. You need to correctly present the meaning, and you need to cite the source accurately. Sometimes it is difficult to try to work with many different ideas, but remember that your professor is very familiar with many of the ideas and sources you'll use and can help you work out how best to present them.

What is the difference between MLA and APA styles in paraphrases?

Like direct quotations, the only difference between APA and MLA styles is the citation at the end.

Example: parenthetical citation, MLA

MLA style includes the name of the author and the page number. This example shows a block quotation.

> Yet in California, the bloodiest drama in the settlement of the West took place. a brutal disruption and destruction so devastating that by the 1870's many native groups were extinct. (Secrest xi)

Example: parenthetical citation, APA

APA style includes the name of the author and the date of publication. This example shows a block quotation.

> Yet in California, the bloodiest drama in the settlement of the West took place, a brutal disruption and destruction so devastating that by the 1870's many native groups were extinct. (Secrest, 2003)

Provide the complete information in your Works Cited or References list at the conclusion of your paper.

Knowledge Check: True or False?

1. Keeping the writing style of the original passage when you paraphrase is appropriate as long as you change most of the words.

2. Correct paraphrasing includes a citation for the original source after the paraphrased passage.
3. A paraphrase should be roughly the same length as the original.

Answers

1. (False) This is a common mistake students make because they don't know the rules and they lack confidence in their own writing ability. You should restate the writer's idea in your own words.
2. (True) Always acknowledge when you've used ideas from someone else, no matter whether it's a clause, sentence, or paragraph.
3. (True) The paraphrase restates another person's idea in your own words.

5
Summarizing

What is a summary?

A **summary** condenses the idea of the original author while retaining the message of the original passage. A summary enables you to comment briefly on another writer's ideas and to express how they relate to your own ideas. Summarizing shortens the length of the original passage, whereas paraphrasing nearly matches the original in length.

Tips

DO
1. Be accurate to the original meaning.
2. Cite the original source.
3. Make your summary significantly shorter than the original.
4. Use your own words and explain how the writer's idea relates to yours.

DON'T
1. Copy the original writing style; use your own.
2. Replace the original words with synonyms.
3. Change the meaning of a passage.

35

To summarize another writer's passage, read it several times—taking notes if necessary—to make sure you understand what the writer is saying. It might help to read the passage aloud so you can hear the words. Then say to yourself, "In other words, ..." and complete the thought. If you find that you are using almost as many words to explain or express the thought, then you need to revise it and make it simpler and briefer. Reduce the original passage to its basic idea. And make sure to explain for your reader how the writer's idea relates to the point you are making in your paper.

Sample summary

Original work

> Polls show that large majorities of Americans believe that anyone who works hard can succeed, and even higher percentages of Americans say they admire people who get rich by their own efforts. Those who fall behind, meanwhile, are often blamed for their misery. In a typical recent survey finding, three quarters of Americans agreed with the statement that if a person is poor, their own "lack of effort" is to blame. In other words, Americans tend to make moral judgments about people based upon their level of economic success. Everybody loves a winner, the saying goes, and nowhere is that more true than in America. Winners are seen as virtuous, as people to admire and emulate. Losers get the opposite treatment for their own good, mind you. As Marvin Olasky, ... has said: "An emphasis on freedom should also include a willingness to step away for a time and let those who have dug their own hole 'suffer the

consequences of their misconduct.'" The
prevalence of a sink-or-swim mentality in the
United States is unique among Western
democracies, as is the belief that individuals have
so much control over their destiny. Elsewhere
people are more apt to believe that success or
failure is determined by circumstances beyond
individual control. Scholars attribute the difference
in outlook to the "exceptionalism" of American
and, especially to the American Dream ethos that
dominates U.S. culture - an ethos at once intensely
optimistic and brutally unforgiving. (Callahan 124-
25)

Incorrect Summary

Polls show that large majorities of Americans
believe that anyone who works hard can
succeed, and even higher percentages of
Americans say they admire people who get
rich by their own efforts. Winners are seen as
virtuous, as people to admire and emulate.
Elsewhere people are more apt to believe that
success or failure is determined by
circumstances beyond individual control.

The above summary was created using the auto-
summarize feature of Word set for 25 percent. It
selects key sentences from the original document and
puts those sentences together to form an abbreviated
copy. (Note that the auto-summarize feature is

intended for writers to provide summaries of their own work, not the work of others.) This is not an acceptable summary because it is entirely copied, word for word. It is plagiarism. It does not change the writing style of the original author, nor does it give credit with a correct citation to indicate the source. Additional problems with this method of summary may be the altering of the original meaning of the piece. Note that the original piece was about the difference between how Americans view winners and losers, but the summary does not mention how losers are viewed. That thesis has not been mentioned in the summary. It is important to connect a summary to the point you fire making in your paper and the reason why you referred to the source you are summarizing.

Correct summary

> According to Callahan, American culture, unlike other Western democracies, takes the moral perspective that success is the result of individual effort. According to polls, a person's success is considered to be a product of his or her labor and thus deserved. Conversely, a person's poverty or failure is viewed as the outcome of his or her lack of sufficient effort and therefore also deserved (124-25).

In the correct summary, the ideas of the original passage are maintained, but the style of writing is different from the original passage. The summary is shorter than the original. The summary conveys the main points of the original, but it does not copy full sentences or pull out words and substitute them with synonyms. It still uses some of the words from the original to accurately present the author's ideas. When you use a summary is a paper, make sure it clearly addresses your thesis or argument and that you cite it correctly.

Knowledge Check: True or False?

1. You can keep the writing style of the original passage when you summarize as long as you significantly shorten the length and leave out some of the original.
2. Correct summarizing includes a citation for the original source next to the summarized passage.
3. A summary should convey the same meaning as the original.

Answers

1. (False) A summary should be in your own words and writing style but convey the message of the original. Do not use autosummarize for someone else's work because it is just an abridged copy.
2. (True) Always acknowledge when you've used ideas from someone else, no matter whether it's a clause, sentence or paragraph, paraphrase or summary.

3. (True) Do not alter the meaning, just express
    it concisely and in your own words.

6
Listing the Works Cited: MLA Documentation

MLA documentation style is most commonly used in courses in the humanities. As you draft your paper and decide how to use your final sources, you will assemble a Works-Cited page to present at the end of your paper, and you will need to format that list of works cited and present that list at the end of your paper. This chapter presents the basics of how to format your Works-Cited items in MLA style. You can find more detailed examples in your textbook, from your school's library or writing center, and from electronic resources such as those listed in Chapter 9.

Tip

Always check with your instructor for the documentation style that he or she requires.

Content of citations

The basic information for a citation in MLA style includes the following:

- Author name.
- Title of article, essay, book, or Web site.
- Publisher information.
- Year of publication.
- Place or form of publication.

Basic format of citations

Follow these basic conventions to create your Works-Cited page:

- Arrange all citations in alphabetical order by the author's last name.
- Arrange authors' names in a multiple-author work exactly as they appear in the source.
- Reverse the first author's name so that the last name appears first.
- Double-space your list of references, the way you double-space your paper.
- Indent the second and subsequent lines of a citation by 1/2 inch or 5 spaces, so the author's name always appears by itself at the left margin.
- Include in your list of Works-Cited only the works that your paper refers to.

Always check with your course instructor for the preferred citation style. (See Chapter 9 for sources of citation styles for specific subject areas such as mathematics, biology, physics, and so on.)

Citing books

The basic MLA style of citation for a book is as follows:

- Author last name first, first name followed by a period.

- Book Title underlined, followed by a period.
- City of publication followed by a colon.
- Publisher's name followed by a comma. Use only the first name of the publisher, and abbreviate University Press to UP.
- Year of publication followed by a period

Example: book with a single author

Maguire, Gregory. <u>Wicked: The Life and Times of the Wicked Witch of the West</u>. New York: Harper, 1995.

Examples: book with multiple authors

When you are citing a book that has two or three authors, list them in the order that they appear on the title page. Invert the first author's name but not the names of the second or third author. Separate all the authors by commas.

For a book by four or more authors, MLA allows the listing to include all authors listed in order or just the first author followed by the Latin words et al. (which is short for *et alii*, meaning "and others"). Check with your instructor about the form that he or she prefers.

A book by two authors

Norman, Michael, and Beth Scott. <u>Historic Haunted America</u>. New York: Tor, 1995.

A book by four or more authors

Kauffman, James, Mark Mostert, Stanley Trent, and

      Daniel Hallahan. <u>Managing Classroom</u>

      <u>Behavior</u>. Boston: Allyn, 2002.

or

 Kauffman, James, et al. <u>Managing Classroom</u>

      <u>Behavior</u>. Boston: Allyn, 2002.

Citing articles or essays

You might use an article from a periodical or an essay from an anthology. While the basic structure of citations for articles is the same as for books, there are some significant differences. You need to list both the title of the article or essay and the journal or book that it was published in.

Example: essay in an anthology

The information in a citation of a source from an anthology follows this order:

- Author of the article or essay (last name first) followed by a period.
- "Title of the article or essay" in quotation marks, followed by a period.
- <u>Title of the Book</u> underlined, followed by a period.

- Comp. (for Compiled by) or Ed. (for Edited by).
- Author of the book (first name first), followed by a period.
- City followed by a colon.
- Publisher followed by a comma.
- Year followed by a period.
- Page range (hyphenated) followed by a period.

Anson, Chris. "Taking Off." <u>Finding Our Way: A Writing Teacher's Sourcebook</u>. Ed. Wendy Bishop and Deborah Coxwell Teague. Boston: Houghton, 2005. 44-51.

For citations from an anthology or magazine, always include the page numbers.

Example: article from a magazine

Magazine or journal articles include the month of publication in the citation. Note the abbreviated month and the colon following the year.

Myers, Michaela. "Pole Results." <u>Horse Illustrated</u> Feb. 2005: 68-74.

Example: article from a journal

Note the volume number following the journal title, the year in parentheses, the colon following the year, and the inclusive page numbers.

Paulos, Lyn. "Sexuality in Women: Feminism in

    Conflict." <u>Women's Studies Weekly</u> 1 (2000):

    15-20.

Citing online sources

Provide the following information for online sources:

- Author (if available).
- Title of Web page.
- Title of full work (if available).
- Date of work (if available) .
- File number (if available).
- Date that you accessed it.
- URL or Web address.

Example: online citation

The MLA citation shows the author's full name and the date after the title. Note that the year of publication is followed by a period, that the date of access is inverted and abbreviated and that no punctuation follows it, that the URL is put in angle brackets, that the line break of the URL falls after a slash, and that a period follows the URL.

Warlick, David. "Landmarks Citation Machine: <u>The</u>

    <u>Landmark Project</u>. 2000.19 Mar. 2005 <http://

    www.landmarkproject.com/citationmachinelind

    ex.php>.

Example: online citation, no author

If the Web site does not have an author or organization listed, then list the title of the Web site. Include the date of publication if available and the date of access. Some Web sites are sponsored or maintained by universities or companies and do not list authors for their Web materials. If that is the case, list the university or company name in the author space of the citation.

DSPS Policies and Procedures. 2003. Santa Barbara
    City College. 3 Jan. 2004
    <http://www.sbcc.edu/dsps/>.

Example: online citation, article from a database

Seithler, Dana. "Unnatural Selection: Mothers, Eugenic
    Feminism, and Charlotte Perkins Gilman's
    Regeneration Narratives." American Quarterly
    55.1 (2003): 61-88. Project Muse. 28 Apr.
    2006. http://muse.jhu.edu/search/pia.cgi.

Example: MLA Works-Cited page

Works Cited

Anson, Chris. "Taking Off." Finding Our Way: A Writing
    Teacher's Sourcebook. Ed. Wendy Bishop and

Deborah Coxwell Teague. Boston: Houghton, 2005. 44-51.

DSPS Policies and Procedures. 2003. Santa Barbara City College. 3 Jan. 2004 <http://www.sbcc.edu/dspsl>.

Kauffman, James, Mark Mostert, Stanley Trent, and Daniel Hallahan. Managing Classroom Behavior. Boston: Allyn, 2002.

Maguire, Gregory. Wicked: The Life and Times of the Wicked Witch of the West. New York: Harper, 1995.

Myers, Michaela. "Pole Results." Horse Illustrated Feb. 2005: 68-74.

Norman, Michael, and Beth Scott. Historic Haunted America. New York: Tor, 1995.

Paulos, Lyn. "Sexuality in Women: Feminism in Conflict." Women's Studies Weekly 1 (2000): 15-20.

Warlick, David. "Landmarks Citation Machine." The Landmark Project. 2000. 19 Mar. 2005 <http:" www.landmarkproject.comlcitationmachine/index.php> .

Knowledge Check: True or False?

1.   Works Cited should be single-spaced.

2. Only works actually cited in the body of the
    paper should be listed in the Works-Cited
    pages.
3. Works Cited should be listed in alphabetical
    order by author's last name.
4. Each reference item can be provided in any
    style (MLA, APA, etc.) as long as it's
    complete.

Answers

1. (False) All references should be double-
    spaced.
2. (True)
3. (True)
4. (False) All of the references should follow the
    style used in the body of the paper. The choice
    of style is determined by the academic subject
    (unless instructed otherwise by your
    professor).

7
Creating a References Page: APA Documentation

Content of citations

The basic information for a citation in APA style includes the following:

- Author name.
- Title of article, essay, book, or Web site.
- Publisher information.
- Year of publication.
- Place or form of publication.

Basic format of citations

Follow these basic conventions to create your References list:

- Arrange all citations in alphabetical order by the author's last name.
- Arrange authors' names in a multiple-author work exactly as they appear in the source.
- Reverse the first author's name so that the last name appears first.
- Double-space your list of references, the way you double-space your paper.
- Indent the second and subsequent lines of a citation by 1/2 inch or 5 spaces, so the author's name always appears by itself at the left margin.

- Include in your list of references only the works that your paper refers to.

Always check with your course instructor for the preferred citation style. (See Chapter 9 for sources of citation styles for specific subject areas such as mathematics, biology, physics, and so on.)

Citing books

APA style is used in many social science courses such as psychology, sociology, and political science. The APA References list contains the same information as the MLA works-cited page, but it formats the content differently, putting more emphasis on the date of publication. The basic APA style of citation for a book is as follows:

Author, last name first, then first initial, followed by a period. For a work by more than one author, invert all names, use initials instead of first names, and insert an ampersand (&) before the last author.

- Year of publication in parentheses, followed by a period.
- Book title italicized (capitalize the first word of the title, the first word of the subtitle, and any proper nouns), followed by a period.
- City and full publisher's name, separated by a colon and followed by a period.

Example: book

Maguire, G. (1995). *Wicked: The life and times of the Wicked Witch of the West*. New York: HarperCollins.

Citing Articles

The basic APA style of citation for a journal article by a single author is as follows:

- Author last name, and first initial followed by a period. For a work by more than one author, invert all names, use initials instead of first names, and insert an ampersand (&) before the last author.
- Year (in parentheses) with a period.
- Title of article (capitalize only first word and first word after a colon, no quotation marks), followed by a period.
- Title of journal in italics followed by a comma.
- Volume number in italics followed by a comma.
- Full page range of article, followed by a period.

Example: journal article by a single author

Paulos, L. (2000). Sexuality in women: Feminism in conflict. *Women's Studies Weekly*, 1, 15-20.

Example: journal article by two to five authors

Paulos, L., & Walker. K. (2005). Understanding twin
    rivalry: A case study. *Sibling Circular, 10*, 70-
    72.

Menager, R., Herch, S., Lewis, G., & Walker, K.
    (2005). Friends and family. *Relations*, 5, 21-24.

Citing online sources

Provide the following information for online sources:

- Author (if available).
- Title of Web page.
- Title of full work (if available).
- Date of work (if available).
- File number (if available).
- Date that you accessed it.
- URL or Web address.

Example: online citation, no print source

APA electronic citations likewise follow the rules of
normal APA style of formatting such as capitalization,
first initial, year placement, and italics. Note that the
retrieval date is spelled out, that a comma follows it,
and that no punctuation follows the URL. If the URL
extends to more than one line, then break it only after a
slash or a period.

Lee. I. (1998). *A research guide for students:*
    Research, writing, and style guides. Retrieved
    March 19,2005, from

http://www.aresearchguide.com/styleguides.ht
ml

Example: APA online citation, print source

McCabe, D. L., Trevino, L. K., & Butterfield, K. D.

(1999). Academic integrity in honor code and

non-honor code environments: A qualitative

investigation. *Journal of Higher Education*, 70,

211-234. Retrieved May 19, 2003, from

http://www.questia.com/SM.qst

Tip

Always include the date of access, because Web sites often change.

Example: online citation, no author

If the Web site does not have an author or organization listed, then list the title of the Web site. Include the date of publication if available and the date of access. Some Web sites are sponsored or maintained by universities or companies and do not list authors for their Web materials. If that is the case, list the university or company name in the author space of the citation.

DSPS policies and procedures. (2003). Santa Barbara
      City College. Retrieved January 3, 2004, from
      http://www.sbcc.edu/dsps/

Example: online citation, online article from database

Smith, M. (2003, September). Making sense of social
      history. *Journal of Social History, 37*, 165-186.
      Retrieved April 4, 2006 from Project Muse
      database.

Example: APA References list

References

DSPS policies and procedures. (2003). Santa Barbara
      City College. Retrieved January 3, 2004, from
      http://www.sbcc.edu/dsps/
Lee, I. (1998). *A research guide for students:
      Research, writing, and style guides.* Retrieved
      March 19, 2005, from
      http://www.aresearchguide.comlstyleguides.html
Maguire, G. (1995). *Wicked: The life and times of the
      Wicked Witch of the West.* New York:
      HarperCollins.

McCabe, D. L., Trevino, L. K., & Butterfield, K. D.

(1999). Academic integrity in honor code and

non-honor code environments: A qualitative

investigation. *Journal of Higher Education*, 70,

211-234. Retrieved May 19, 2003, from

http://www.questia.comISM.qst

Menager, R., Herch, S., Lewis, G., & Walker, K.

(2005). Friends and family. *Relations*, 5, 21-24.

Paulos, L. (2000). Sexuality in women: Feminism in

conflict. *Women's Studies Weekly*, 1, 15-20.

Paulos, L., & Walker. K. (2005). Understanding twin

rivalry: A case study. *Sibling Circular*, 10, 70-

72.

Knowledge Check: True or False?

1. References should be single-spaced.
2. Only works actually cited in the body of the paper should be listed in the Reference list.
3. References should be listed in alphabetical order by author's last name.
4. Each reference item can be provided in any style (MLA, APA, etc.) as long as it's complete.

Answers

1. (False) All references should be double-spaced.
2. (True)
3. (True)

4. (False) All of the references should follow the style
used in the body of the paper. The choice of style is
determined by the academic subject (unless instructed
otherwise by your professor).

8
Practice Quiz

1. Cheating may include
    a. plagiarizing or copying without attribution.
    b. using an essay or paper from someone who has previously taken the course.
    c. using answers to an exam from someone who has previously taken the course.
    d. all of the above.

2. Plagiarism is
    a. quoting someone else's work and giving credit to them.
    b. using someone else's ideas, work, sentences, research, or information and presenting it as your own.
    c. using original ideas in your written work.
    d. using Web sources.

3. Citation of sources is required
    a. whenever paraphrasing or summarizing another author's idea.
    b. only in the works cited section of your paper.
    c. when using your own ideas in an original paragraph.
    d. a and b.

4. The word paraphrase means
    a. to replace original words with synonyms.
    b. to maintain the writing style of the original author.

   c.   to give an exact idea of the original author's meaning in your own writing style.

   d.   to give a general, but not exact, idea of the original author's meaning.

5. A paragraph is not properly paraphrased when

   a.   only a few words are different.

   b.   you express in your own words the general idea of what the author is saying.

   c.   the sentences have been rearranged but not changed much.

   d.   a and b.

   e.   a and c.

6. Correct summarizing includes

   a.   a copy of the original writing style.

   b.   replacing the original work with synonyms.

   c.   the accurate meaning of the original work but significantly shorter than the original.

   d.   using the autosummarize feature of your word processing program.

7. Citation of sources is required

   a.   when quoting a source in your paper that you use word for word.

   b.   when browsing the Internet.

   c.   when describing another writer's idea in your paper.

   d.   a and c.

8. Over-quoting in your work

   a.   shows you have not synthesized or analyzed the material from your resources.

b. is acceptable because it shows the amount of work and research you have done.
c. means using too many direct quotes from your sources.
d. a and c.
e. a and b.

9. John's paper is based on several different sources, including a research paper from a friend who took the same class last summer. Seeing that his friend's research closely matches his own, does John need to cite his friend in his final draft?

a. No, he just needs to cite the other sources.
b. Yes, anything John consults and incorporates needs to be cited.

10. Look at the original and choose which paraphrase is correct.

Original

Because there are many ways to cheat, and there is temptation to do so, students may assume that this is something that everyone is doing. Surveys of college students show that cheating is a common occurrence, and some students consider it an accomplishment to get away with this type of behavior. These kinds of attitudes and behaviors are unethical and have consequences. (Menager-Beeley 2003)

a. Students can be tempted to cheat by the many resources available to them that make it easy. They may believe that a majority of students cheat in some form or another. Surveys done in colleges suggest that cheating is more rampant than once thought and that students see it as a triumph to cheat and not get caught. This shows a serious lack of ethics in behavior and can lead to repercussions from the academic institution. (Menager-Beeley, 2003)

b. Because there are so many different ways to cheat, and temptations for students are great, a lot of students think everyone is doing it. Students surveyed say that cheating is a common occurrence and it is an accomplishment to get away with it. This kind of attitude is unethical and can have some consequences.

Answers:

1. d   2. b   3. a   4. c   5. e   6. c   7. d   8. d   9. b   10. a

9
Additional Sources of Information

The following links are subject to change. They were accessed April 24, 2006.

Web sites with information on documentation styles, by discipline

Anthropology
<http://www.aaanet.org/pubs/style_guide.htm>

Legal
< http://www.law.cornell.edu/citation/?>

Physics
<http://www.aip.org/pubservs/style.html>

Free Citation Generators

Landmark's Citation Machine
<http://www.citationmachine.net/>

Style Wizard
<http://www.stylewizard.com/>

Reference Tracking, Subscriptions, and Free Trials

Easy Bib
<http://easybib.com/>

RefWorks
<http://www.refworks.com>

Links for Articles on Plagiarism

Center for Academic Integrity
<http://www.academicintegrity.org/links.asp>

Plagiarism.org
<http://www.plagiarism.org/articles.html>

University of Indiana
<http://www.indiana.edu/~istd/definition.html>

Print Resources, Style Guides
American Psychological Association. *Concise Rules of APA Style*. Washington: APA, 2005. <http://www.apa.org/books/>.

Gibaldi, Joseph. *The MLA Style Guide for Writers of Research Papers*. 6th ed. New York: MLA, 2003. <http://www.mla.org/store/>.

Huth, Edward J. *Scientific Style and Format: The CBE Manual for Authors, Editors and Publishers*. 6th ed. New York: Cambridge UP, 1994. < http://www.councilscienceeditors.org/ publications/style.cfm> .

University of Chicago Press Staff. *The Chicago Manual of Style*. 15th ed. Chicago: U of Chicago P, 2003. <http://www.chicagomanualofstyle.org/ about.html>.

10
Works Cited

Byrne, Robert. The 2,548 Best Things Anybody Ever Said. New York: Galahad, 1996. Sec. 453.

Covey, Stephen. The Seven Habits of Highly Effective People. New York: Simon, 1989. 97, 186.

Melville, Herman. "Quotation 4797" Cole's Quotables. 30 Mar. 2005 <http://www.quotationspage.com/quotes/Herman _Melville/>.

Potter, W. James. "Is Media Violence Harmful to Children?" Taking Sides: Clashing on Controversial Psychological Issue. 13th ed. Ed. Brent Slife. New York: McGraw, 2004. 306.

Secrest, William B. When the Great Spirit Died: Destruction of the California Indians, 1850-1860. Sanger: Word Dancer, 2003.

Tavares, Jess. "Returning Students." Scholarship essay. May 2002.

VanderMey, et. al. The College Writers Handbook. Boston: Houghton, 2006. 486.

Weeks, Dudley. The Eight Essential Steps to Conflict Resolution. 2002. New York: Tarcher-Penguin, 1994. 33.

Zaharoff, Howard. "A Writer's Guide to Fair Use in
        Copyright Law." Writers Digest Jan. 2001. 3
        Mar. 2005
        <http://www.writersdigest.com/articles/zaharof
        f_fair_copyright_law .asp>.